1. Introduction

The Telecommunications Act of 1996 (henceforth the 1996 Act) established a framework under which local telephone markets in the United States would be opened to competition. This necessitated the development of an inter-carrier compensation regime for inter-network traffic.[1] This regime affects networks' retail prices, which affects network usage and therefore efficiency.

Under the 1996 Act all local exchange carriers (LECs) are required "… to establish reciprocal compensation arrangements for the transport and termination of telecommunications."[2] The reciprocal compensation guidelines developed by the FCC established a "calling party's network pays" (CPNP) regime, in which a calling party's (or originating) network pays the called party's (or terminating) network a termination fee equal to the Total Element Long Run Incremental Cost (TELRIC) of the traffic-sensitive facilities of the terminating network used to complete the call.[3] The rationale for this policy, which effectively imposes the entire cost of the call on the originating network,[4] is that the originating network imposes a cost on the terminating network, and therefore the originating network must fully compensate the terminating network for this cost.[5]

The main purpose of this paper is to point out that both parties to a call often share the value of the minutes of conversation consumed,[6] and in such cases it is efficient for them to share

---

[1] The 1996 Act imposes on *all* telecommunications carriers "the duty to … interconnect directly or indirectly with the facilities and equipment of other telecommunications carriers…"; see 47 U.S.C. § 251(a)(1). It also imposes more detailed interconnection requirements on local exchange carriers. (See 47 U.S.C. §251(b)(1)) and incumbent local exchange carriers. (see 47 U.S.C. §251(c)(2)).
[2] See 47 U.S.C. §251(b)(5). The 1996 Act contemplates that such terms would be negotiated between carriers.
[3] See FCC (1996) at 674-703. In the case of switching (and tandem switching) TELRIC is typically calculated as a forward-looking long run per minute average cost, which is the total forward-looking annualized lifetime cost of building and operating a switch divided by the number of minutes the switch processes in a year.
[4] Whether the calling party actually bears the entire cost depends on whether his carrier can set rates to reflect termination fees. In the United States long distance usage rates typically reflect termination rate levels, while local carriers are constrained by regulators to charge flat-rated local rates.
[5] See, for example, *Iowa Utilities Board, v FCC*, No. 96-3321 Slip op. at 8 (8th Cir. Jul. 18, 2000). See also FCC(1996) at 1057.
[6] Squire (1973) and Willig (1979) raised such issues in the context of regulating a monopoly provider of telephony. Such ideas, seemed to have been ignored in later discussions of interconnection between competing networks, until a recent works by Kim and Lim (2001) and Doyle and Smith (1998). In work developed currently but independently of this paper, Hermalin and Katz (2000) address issues similar to those in this paper.

the costs.[7] I show that parties to a call should bear the incremental cost of a minute in the same proportion that they share the value. For example, if the calling party receives 65% of the value of a minute, efficiency requires him to bear 65% of the cost. Thus, contrary to much of the existing literature, I show that requiring the terminating network to bear some of the incremental termination costs so that it will impose this cost on the called party can be efficient.[8]

An implication of this analysis is that customers should not be viewed as purchasing completed calls, but rather as contracting for the use of specific facilities, which must be combined appropriately to complete a call. The calling party incurs the cost of some of these facilities, and the called party incurs the cost of others.[9]

Much of my formal analysis assumes customers share equally in the value of a call, and shows that local networks interconnecting at a specific point and exchanging traffic at this point on a bill and keep basis produces a more efficient equilibrium than the equilibrium produced under CPNP. I call this regime meet-point bill and keep (MBAK).[10] In fact if carriers have access to the same technology and customers share the value of calls equally, MBAK results in first best network utilization[11] while CPNP does not.

---

[7] It is therefore not helpful to think of the originating network as imposing a cost on the terminating network. Rather, because the called party is a willing participant in a call, he can be viewed as imposing the cost on his own network and, therefore, should be responsible for the cost.
  It may be argued that many customers receive calls from telemarketers for which they receive little or no benefit. However, such customers have the option of hanging up almost instantaneously, so such calls in principle could account for relatively few minutes consumed by customers.

[8] See for example Laffont, Rey, and Tirole (1998); Laffont and Tirole (2000); and Economides, Lopomo, and Woroch (1996), who argue that having the calling party pay all of the incremental costs associated with a call is efficient. See also 47 U.S.C. § 252(d)(2)(A).

[9] While it is not customary in the US for called parties to be charged for usage on wireline networks, many wireless carriers charge their customers for airtime when they receive calls.

[10] This is consistent with the FCC proposal outlined in Atkinson and Barnekov (2000).

[11] This assumes parties have no other commercial interaction. Allowing side payments between the calling and called parties implies that carrier-to-carrier payments are redundant. Any allocation can be obtained with three contracts, one between each carrier and her customer and one between customers can generate all possible allocations. Salop (1990) makes a similar point in the context of networks of shared Automated Teller Machines (ATMs). See also Besen, Manning and Mitchell (1978) and Gans and King (2001).

I concentrate on bill and keep, not because a zero inter-carrier compensation rate is likely to give rise to theoretically optimal usage levels, but because the optimal rate may be very close to zero. Thus, a zero inter-carrier compensation rate may generate very small distortions in usage, while the alternative, which is likely to be a CPNP regime, may create more significant inefficiencies and distortions.[12] Thus, as a policy matter, society may be better off accepting the small usage distortions of bill and keep, rather than the distortions arising from CPNP. Therefore, my results regarding MBAK should be viewed as benchmarks.

There are several reasons to study the efficiency property of inter-carrier compensation rates. First, though the 1996 Act requires carriers to negotiate interconnection agreements, virtually all agreements between incumbent local exchange carriers (ILECs) and competitive local exchange carriers (CLECs) have been settled by arbitration. So these results can aid regulators in setting rates.[13] Second, even if carriers were to successfully negotiate rates, there is no guarantee that negotiated rates would be efficient. For example Katz, Rosston and Anspacher (1996) and Brennan (1997) explain that carriers might agree on high compensation rates to facilitate collusion. It has also been argued that, because each network is a monopolist with respect to terminating calls to its customers, each has an incentive to set the monopoly rate for that service. While determining the conditions (if any) under which negotiation leads to efficient compensation rates is beyond the scope of this paper,[14] this work helps to characterize efficient rates.

My analysis assumes competing networks provide homogeneous services, eliminating the need to model competing networks as offering differentiated products.[15] This is important because

---

[12] See DeGraba (2002) for a list of problems created by cost-based inter-carrier compensation. These include: a) regulators have less information about network costs than carriers who may over- report costs to obtain higher regulated prices; b) allowing carriers to recover only traffic sensitive costs may cause carriers to invest in technologies with high traffic-sensitive costs, even if these are not the cost minimizing technologies; c) termination charges endow customers that are net terminators of minutes with rents, creating incentives for carriers to engage in rent-seeking behavior.
[13] ILECs have little incentive to reach agreements with entrants, since this would facilitate competitive entry.
[14] See for example Brennan (1997).
[15] See for example Kim and Lim (2001) and Laffont, Rey and Tirole (1998).

one issue in analyzing inter-carrier compensation rates is whether they create tipping equilibria. Differentiated products models create a natural tendency for different customers to gravitate toward different networks, which will tend to mask the tipping effects that can be caused by inappropriate termination charges.

There are two recent works that considers the idea that called parties receive benefits from a call. Kim and Lim (2001) looks at the case where two networks agree on an termination rate, and analyze how this rate will differ between the case in which customers can be charged a usage fee for receiving calls and the case in which they cannot. They do not focus on finding an optimal termination charge. Doyle and Smith (1998) examines how the "receiver pays" principle affects the prices of mobile customers, but does not focus on the optimal termination charge.

The paper is organized as follows. Section 2 explains why it is efficient for customers to share costs in proportion to the value they receive from a call. Section 3 provides a formal model showing that bill and keep can be more efficient than the existing inter-carrier compensation regimes. Section 4 discusses extensions. Concluding remarks are in Section 5.

2. Optimal cost sharing between calling and called party

This section shows that if customers share the value of a minute of calling, they consume the optimal level when they jointly pay a per minute price equal to the marginal cost of that minute, and each customer pays a proportion of this price equal to the proportion of the value he receives from that minute. The intuition behind this result is similar to the intuition behind the Lindahl equilibrium for the provision of a public good.[16] In a Lindahl equilibrium the optimal output level occurs where the sum of the marginal benefit of each customer from the last unit of a public good equals the marginal cost of producing that unit. In this paper a call can be viewed as a public good jointly consumed by the calling and called parties.

---

[16] I am grateful to an anonymous referee for pointing out the public goods interpretation of these results.

I model a call as requiring the use of a switch that serves the calling party, a switch that serves the called party and a trunk that connects the two switches, each of which generates marginal per minute costs. This structure applies both to calls between parties on the same network, which I refer to as on-net calls, and to parties served by different networks, which I refer to as off-net calls.[17]

Let $V(m)$ be the *total* value of the mth minute of calling consumed by the two parties. Let p_o be the price facing the calling (originating) party and p_t be the price facing the called (terminating) party. Let c represent the marginal cost of providing a minute of calling.

Proposition 1. Suppose that $V(m)$ is a decreasing function of m, and that the calling party receives λ of the value of each minute while the called party receives $(1-\lambda)$ of the value. Then the parties consume the efficient level of minutes if the calling party faces a price equal to λc and the called party faces $(1-\lambda)c$. This is the only set of prices that sum to c that yield efficient consumption.

Proof:

A minute of calling is completed if and only if both parties to the call voluntarily engage in the minute. The calling party is willing to engage in minute m' if $\lambda V(m') \geq p_o$ and the called party is willing to engage in minute m' if $(1-\lambda)V(m') \geq p_t$. Let m^* be the efficient level of calling; i.e., m^* is the minute for which $V(m^*) = c$. Setting $p_o = \lambda c$ and $p_t = (1-\lambda)c$ implies that m^* is the last minute in which each party will engage.

To see that no other prices that sum to c yield efficient consumption levels, suppose the calling party faced a price in excess of λc. Then he would consume fewer minutes than is optimal.

---

[17] The wireline loop connecting the customer to the switch typically involves no traffic-sensitive costs. Society's overall cost of having multiple networks can be no higher than the costs of having a monopoly network when all switches are used to capacity. To see this start with a monopoly local network and then let it divest some of its facilities to a competitor. On average off-net calls will have a slightly higher expected trunking cost than on-net calls, since some on-net calls occur between customers on the same switch and require no trunking. I abstract from this minor cost difference.

Suppose the calling party faced a price less than λc. Then the called party would face a price in excess of $(1-\lambda)c$, which would cause him to consume fewer minutes than is optimal. *QED*

This result applies to both on-net and off-net calls. Thus, if on-net and off-net calls have the same cost, efficiency requires that they have the same price for each party. This is not surprising since both must be priced at marginal cost. Proposition 1 implies two sufficient conditions for efficiency. The first is that $p_o + p_t = c$. The second is that $p_o/p_t = \lambda/(1-\lambda)$.

Proposition 1 focuses only on prices that sum to c. It can be shown that to obtain efficient consumption only one party must face the efficient price while the other must face a price no greater than the efficient price.[18] Because each party has "veto power" over continuing joint consumption, prices must be such that neither party vetoes consumption before the efficient level is reached, but at least one party vetoes consumption at any level beyond the efficient level.

I now ask what compensation rate results in customers facing efficient prices. Let c_o be the originating network's marginal cost of providing its portion of an off-net call and c_t be the terminating network's analogous costs (so that $c_o + c_t = c$). Let a be the termination rate (or "access" charge) paid by the calling party's network to the called party's network. The calling party's network's effective cost is $c_o + a$, and the called party's network's effective cost is $c_t - a$. Assume that competition causes carriers to set usage rates equal to their incremental cost.[19] Proposition 2 presents the optimal termination rate.

Proposition 2. Suppose competition results in each carrier setting usage rates equal to her network's effective marginal cost. The efficient termination rate is $a^* = (\lambda-1)c_o + \lambda c_t$.

---

[18] When the inequality holds strictly, prices will not sum to c.
[19] Propositions 3 and 4 provide conditions under which carriers set rates equal to costs.

Proof:

Efficiency will be achieved if the calling party's network sets a price of $\lambda(c_o + c_t)$ and the called party's network sets $(1-\lambda)(c_o + c_t)$. If carriers set usage rates equal to their effective marginal cost, then the calling party's network sets this price if a^* satisfies $c_o + a^* = \lambda(c_o + c_t)$. Since net access charges are 0, this condition also implies the called party's network bears the remaining $(1-\lambda)(c_o + c_t)$ and charges this to the called party. Thus, $a^* = (\lambda-1)c_o + \lambda c_t$. QED

Proposition 2 presents several interesting implications. First the optimal interconnection charge allocates costs to each network so that the fraction of the marginal cost of producing a minute is equal to the fraction of the value its customer receives from the minute. That is, under a^*, the effective cost of the originating network is $\lambda(c_o + c_t.)$, and the effective cost of the terminating network is $(1-\lambda)(c_o + c_t.)$.

Second, $a^* = 0$ if $\lambda/(1-\lambda) = c_o/c_t$. Thus, MBAK is optimal when the proportion of the value of each minute received by the calling party is equal to the proportion of the cost incurred by his network. The most obvious example of this occurs if customers share the value of a call equally and their networks use the same technology. In this case, the appropriate bill and keep arrangement is MBAK, in which carriers exchange traffic on a bill and keep basis at the "midpoint" of the trunk connecting the networks.[20] In this case each carrier would incur its own switching cost and half of the trunking costs.

Third, a^* could be negative, if for example $\lambda < \frac{1}{2}$ and $c_o = c_t$, or $\lambda = \frac{1}{2}$ and $c_o > c_t$.

Finally, bill and keep is efficient when the marginal cost is zero. This is an obvious but important point because while many telecommunications costs are not traffic-sensitive, they

---

[20] Trunking is viewed as traffic-sensitive (as is switching). So exchanging traffic at the midpoint means each carrier pays half of the cost of operating a single trunk between networks. DeGraba (2002) explains that Central Office Bill and Keep (COBAK) a regime in which the originating network pays all transportation costs could be more efficient if the calling party receives more of the benefit of a call than the called party.

nonetheless are recovered on a traffic-sensitive basis. To the extent that termination rates represent fixed costs that are recovered on a per minute basis, my results indicate those termination rates are too high and could inefficiently reduce network usage.[21]

Finally, the optimal termination rate applies to individual calls and is completely independent of the total amount of traffic originated on one network as opposed to the other. Thus, bill and keep regimes can be efficient when there is an imbalance of traffic between networks (i.e., when one network originates more traffic than the other). This result contradicts the widely held belief that bill and keep is appropriate only when traffic is balanced.[22]

3. Equilibrium analysis when customers share the value of a call equally

I now present a model in which customers share the value of a call equally. Assuming equal call value significantly reduces the complexity of calculating equilibria. Under this condition, and assuming competing networks have access to the same technology, I show that MBAK maximizes social surplus. (I discuss asymmetries in the next section.)

There are two carriers, 1 and 2, that operate competing interconnected telephone networks. The cost of providing one minute of origination for each network is 1 cent, and the cost of a minute of termination is also 1 cent.[23] A completed minute of phone conversation between two customers requires one unit of origination and one of termination. This is true both for on-net and off-net calls.

There are two customers A, and B. In this example let $V = 5 - m$ be the joint valuation curve of minutes of phone conversation between A and B, where m is the number of minutes, and V is the total value received by the two parties for the mth minute of calling. Each party receives

---

[21] Many costs are really capacity costs and are properly viewed as peak-load costs. Yet peak-load costs are often averaged over all minutes (peak and off-peak) and recovered on a per minute basis from all minutes.
[22] See for example FCC (1996), paras. 1057-58.
[23] This is consistent with assuming origination and termination each require a minute if switching and a unit of trunking used in fixed proportions.

half of the value of each minute consumed. Thus, for example, the calling party and called party each receive a value of 1 from the 3rd minute of conversation.

Initially, one phone call is made. It lasts as long as both customers choose to continue the call. That is, once the call is made, each customer participates in the call as long as his private value of an incremental minute exceeds his private cost of engaging in that minute. Once a party reaches the point where his private benefit equals his private cost, he hangs up.

The initial calling party is chosen randomly. Assume that A will be the calling party with probability 2/3 and that B will be the calling party with probability 1/3.[24] It is perhaps useful to think that there is some information that will be valuable to both parties, but that only one of the two parties learns the information. When he learns it, he calls the other party and informs him.[25] I assume callers have different exogenously determined probabilities of originating a call that are independent of prices, because such situations exist in practice, and because termination charges affect the way carriers compete for such customers.[26]

If the call ends at a point at which the called party's marginal valuation of a minute exceeds his price of initiating a call, then he makes a call to the initial caller. The call will be completed if the initial caller's private value from additional conversation is greater than his private cost of receiving the call.[27] (Note that if both customers face the same cost of origination

---

[24] All of the results of the propositions in this section would hold if each customer were to initiate the first call with probability ½. Adding this asymmetry highlights the fact that otherwise equivalent customers are treated differently when there is an inefficient termination fee imposed by the government.

[25] For example restaurants and mail-order houses receive more calls than they make because the customer has better information on when it is time to order such services than does the vendor. There certainly are cases where different rates facing two parties will affect who originates a call. Perhaps the most important example is the so called "call turnaround scenario," where a call made from overseas to the United States will be instantly terminated and replaced by a call made from the United States to the initial originating number, so that U.S. origination retail rates, which are significantly less expensive than overseas rates will apply.

[26] Because the ILEC initially serves all customers, CLECs can and do target customers who terminate more minutes than they originate. At this writing, virtually all CLECs are net terminators of inter network minutes.

[27] This last assumption is important for the existence of a pure strategy equilibrium. Note that in a symmetric equilibrium it will never be the case that the randomly chosen originator does not make the call and the other party does. Thus, this is an assumption about off-equilibrium behavior that never occurs. An alternative formulation is to assume that each call lasts one second. Nature picks A to initiate each call with probability 2/3 and B to initiate it with probability 1/3. A customer initiate the call iff his private benefit

and the same cost of termination, then only one call will be made in equilibrium.) For every off-net minute originated by its subscribers, the originating network pays the terminating network a per minute termination charge, denoted a, which is set by the regulator.

Given this structure, I present the following game, played among the carriers and the customers. The regulator sets a exogenously. Carriers observe a, and in Stage 1 announce their per minute usage prices. They can set four different usage prices; $p_{iof} \equiv$ carrier i's price for originating off-net minutes, $p_{ion} \equiv$ carrier i's price for originating on-net minutes, $p_{itf} \equiv$ carrier i's price for terminating off-net minutes, and $p_{itn} \equiv$ carrier i's price for terminating on-net minutes; $i \in \{1, 2\}$, subscripts o and t represent "origination" and "termination" respectively, and n and f represent "on-net" and "off-net," respectively. Let q_{iof}, q_{ion}, q_{itf} and q_{itn} be the corresponding quantities of these different minutes sold by carrier i.

In Stage 2 each customer observes the prices and subscribes to one network. This choice is made to maximize the customer's expected consumer surplus from consuming minutes of conversation given the prices and the subscription decision of the other customer. The existence of network externalities makes the customers' choice of networks non-trivial.[28]

Once customers have chosen their networks, the remainder of the game is played out mechanically. Nature chooses which customer initiates the call, and the customers engage in all minutes of conversation for which their private value (weakly) exceeds their private cost.

The profit for each carrier is the revenue she receives from her customers plus the access revenue she receives, less her cost of providing switching and the access payments she makes. Formally, $\Pi_i = p_{ion} q_{ion} + p_{itn} q_{itn} + (p_{iof} - a) q_{iof} + (p_{itf} + a) q_{itf} - (1)(q_{ion} + q_{itn} + q_{iof} + q_{itf})$.

The payoff to each customer is the consumer surplus he receives, which is the sum of the value he receives from each minute of calling less the price of that minute.

---

exceeds his private cost of initiating the call. Nature continually chooses one or the other to initiate calls until no more calls will be completed regardless of which caller is chosen to initiate the call.

[28] The possibility that on-net and off-net prices could be different means that the value a customer receives from his choice of network depends on the subscription choice of the other customer.

I consider only subgame perfect Nash equilibria.

Proposition 3. If $a = 0$ then there exists an equilibrium in which $p_{iof} = p_{ion} = p_{itf} = p_{itn} = 1$. This equilibrium is efficient.

Proof: The formal proof is provided in Appendix A.

This result is interesting for several reasons. First, it shows that if customers share the value of a call equally and competing carriers have the same costs of providing service, then an MBAK access regime ($a = 0$) yields first best equilibrium prices. As noted above, this efficiency occurs even though *traffic is unbalanced*. That is, in expectation A originates more minutes than he terminates.[29] Thus, the network that serves him originates more off-net minutes than it terminates.[30] This result shows that traffic balance has no effect on the efficiency of the inter-carrier compensation regime. Rather, it is the division of the value of a call between customers and the costs between networks that determines the efficient access regime.

Second, this example shows that the optimal customer strategy choice is not the trivial "buy from the lowest price seller" choice of the "private goods" Bertrand game. Because of a carrier's ability to set off-net usage rates, one carrier can impose a negative externality on customers who subscribe to its competitor's network. This can lead to multiple subgame perfect customer subscription choices. For example, suppose Carrier 1 sets all usage rates equal to 1 cent per minute while Carrier 2 sets infinite off-net usage rates and on-net origination rates equal to $1 + \delta$ cents per minute and on-net termination rates at $1 - \delta/2$ cents per minute. There are two subgame perfect responses for customers. In one both customers subscribe to network 1 and in the other

---

[29] In this model I have not allowed carriers to price discriminate between A and B. In DeGraba (2000) I have allowed for such price discrimination and find exactly the same equilibrium. Thus, even if carriers can identify which customer terminates more traffic, bill and keep remains the efficient inter-carrier compensation regime.

[30] See, for example, FCC (1996) at 1113, where the FCC ruled that bill and keep arrangements are allowable only if traffic between two carriers is balanced. See also Sidak and Spulber (1996).

both customers subscribe to network 2.[31] Thus, in specifying an equilibrium, one must specify equilibrium subscription rules for customers as well as prices for carriers.

I now show that if $a = 1$, the prices in Proposition 1 cannot be supported in an equilibrium. $a = 1$ is important because it is the CPNP rate, currently imposed by many regulators.

Proposition 4. If $a = 1$, no equilibrium exists with $p_{iof} = p_{ion} = p_{itf} = p_{itn} = 1$.

Proof:

Suppose that carriers set $p_{iof} = p_{ion} = p_{itf} = p_{itn} = 1$. If each customer were to subscribe to each network with any positive probability, each carrier would earn a zero expected profit.

Suppose now that Carrier 2 deviates by setting $p_{2tf} = p_{2tn} = 1 - \varepsilon$, and $p_{2of} = p_{2on} = 1 + \varepsilon$. Then the only subgame perfect continuation is for B, who in expectation will terminate more minutes than he will originate, to subscribe to network 2, and for A, who on average will originate more minutes than he will terminate, to subscribe to network 1. Under this deviation, Carrier 2 in expectation terminates $(2/3)3 + (1/3)\varepsilon$ off-net minutes and originates $(1/3)(3-\varepsilon)$ off-net minutes, and therefore earns a payoff of $(2/3)3(1-\varepsilon +1-1) + (1/3)[(3-\varepsilon)(1+\varepsilon-1-1)+(1-\varepsilon +1-1) \varepsilon] > 0$ for $0 < \varepsilon < 1$. QED

Proposition 4 suggests that if carriers attempt to price efficiently when there is a positive access charge, an arbitrage opportunity arises. Customers who terminate more off-net minutes than they originate generate a positive profit, and customers who originate more off-net minutes than they terminate generate a loss. If the efficient retail prices are set (which effectively averages the total cost across the two customers), a carrier has an incentive to deviate unilaterally in a way that attracts only those customers who terminate traffic by offering a discount for off-net termination and imposing a premium for off-net origination. There currently is a good example of

---

[31] A would prefer the first and B would prefer the second. Note that these prices could not constitute a Nash equilibrium of the overall game. If both customers subscribe to network 2 given these prices, Carrier 2 would earn a strictly positive profit. But Carrier 1's best response would be to charge prices that were ε below those set by Carrier 2, serve both customers and earn a positive profit.

this behavior in telecom markets. Certain entrants into local markets choose to serve primarily Internet Service Providers (ISPs) in order to collect large amounts of termination from the off-net dial-up Internet access these ISPs generate. This is known as the ISP reciprocal compensation problem.[32]

It is of course interesting to ask what kind of equilibrium occurs when $a = 1$.

Proposition 5. When $a = 1$, there are two equilibria in which $p_{iof} = 2$, $p_{itf} = 0$ and $p_{ion} = p_{itn} = 1$. In one equilibrium, both customers subscribe to network 1. In the other, both subscribe to network 2.
Proof: The formal proof is provided in Appendix A.

When customers share equally in the value of a call, it is efficient for them to share the cost equally as well. A positive access charge creates an inefficiency for off-net calls. In particular, it induces carriers to set prices that impose all incremental costs on the calling party. This causes too few minutes of inter-network calling to be consumed. This inefficiency can be eliminated if all customers subscribe to the same network, because the access charge does not affect the carrier's cost of providing on-net calls. Each carrier sets the usage rate for on-net calls at the efficient level, equal to the cost each customer imposes on the network. Thus, because the access charge creates an inefficiency only with respect to calls between customers on different networks, both customers have an incentive to subscribe to the same network. In this model, the positive access charge leads to a tipping equilibrium.[33]

It is interesting to ask what would happen if carriers were not allowed to distinguish between on-net and off-net calls when setting usage rates to customers. Such a constraint will

---

[32] RBOCs report that they paid out $2 billion in termination fees to CLECs serving ISPs in year 2000.
[33] An alternative explanation is to note that if the government were to impose a tax on transactions between vertically related firms, the two firms would vertically integrate to avoid the inefficient tax. In telecommunications an inefficient access charge can cause all customers to join the same network to avoid inefficiently priced inter-carrier services.

have no effect on prices if the regulator sets the efficient termination rate. When a is set efficiently, the unconstrained carriers will charge the same rate for on-net calls as off-net calls. Thus, the constraint has no effect on equilibrium pricing. So if $c_t = c_o = c/2$ then $a^* = (2\lambda -1)c/2$ yields efficient prices for any λ under the constraint.

If a is not set at the efficient level, then, as in Proposition 4, the efficient prices cannot be sustained in equilibrium. To see this, suppose $a = c_1 = c_2 = c/2$, but the calling party receives only ¾ of the benefit of any minute. Then the efficient price for origination is $3c/4$ and the efficient price for termination is $c/4$. However, when a carrier's customer originates an off-net minute, the carrier incurs a cost (including the termination charge) of c, but collects only $3c/4$ in usage fees, and thus loses money. Similarly, when a customer terminates an off-net minute the carrier incurs a cost of $c/2$, but receives revenue (including the termination charge) of $3c/4$, and thus earns a profit. Therefore, at the efficient prices, each carrier would prefer to have B on her network and A on the other network. If carrier 1 were setting the efficient rates, carrier 2 could set $p_{of2} = 3c/4 + \varepsilon$ and $p_{tf2} = c/4 - \varepsilon$. Under these rates B would subscribe to Carrier 2 and A would subscribe to Carrier 1. For ε close to zero, Carrier 2 would earn a strictly positive profit.

The results of this section suggest that when customers share equally in the value of a call and competing networks have the same production costs, it is efficient for networks to exchange traffic on a bill and keep basis. A CPNP regime introduces inefficiencies into the system, which can destabilize the market. In the next section, I show these intuitions are robust vis-à-vis more complete models of competition.

4. Extensions

The model of Section 3 employed several simplifying assumptions. I now explore whether these insights are likely to survive as some of the simplifications are relaxed.

4.1. More than two customers

The model of the previous section assumed that there are only two customers. DeGraba (2000) presents a model that (among other things[34]) replaces A and B with a continuum of customers of type A and a continuum of customers of type B. All results from section 3 hold under this generalization. In particular, when the access charge is zero, carriers set all usage rates equal to 1, as in Proposition 3. Both customer types subscribe randomly to each network. The allocation is first best efficient, and each carrier earns a zero profit. When the access charge equals the switching cost of the terminating network, there are tipping equilibria like those in Proposition 5 above.[35]

4.2. The Allocation of the Value of a Minute is Random

The preceding analysis assumed the calling party receives λ of the value of each minute. It is important to determine how the results generalize to the case where the proportion of the value each party receives varies across minutes. A model with more than two customers and random allocation of the value of each minute would facilitate the analysis in this case. Unfortunately, such a model is beyond the scope of this paper.[36]

I present the following analysis, which suggests that the results of this paper can be extended to the case where the proportion of value received by the parties varies across minutes. There are two networks, 1 and 2, serving a continuum of identical customers, half of whom

---

[34] This model allows for two-part tariffs and accounts for the fact that switching also involves fixed costs. In the extension each A type initiates each call with probability 2/3 and each B type initiates each call with probability 1/3. In such an extension the proportion of calls each type i makes to other i types and the proportion of calls each makes to non-i types must also be specified.

[35] Assuming that A's and B's each originate calls with probability ½ generates a third equilibrium in which half of the customers subscribe to each network. This equilibrium is both inefficient and unstable.

[36] In particular, it is not clear what set of assumptions would be needed in a model in which a equaled the marginal cost of terminating that would lead to a pure strategy equilibrium in which the calling party bore the entire cost of origination and termination for off-net calls, parties shared equally the cost of on-net calls, and some parties subscribe to each network. (DeGraba 2000 provides one such set of assumptions that yields a knife-edge equilibrium.)

subscribe to network 1 and half of whom subscribe to network 2. Each customer talks to the same number of customers on his own network as on the other network. There is a single joint valuation curve that applies to calling between all pairs of customers. The joint valuations of a minute can fall in the interval $[0, v]$. For any given valuation $v' \in [0, v]$, there is a symmetric distribution of the allocation of v' between the calling party and the called party. That is, the proportion of the value the calling party receives is symmetrically distributed over the range $[0, 1]$.[37] Finally, every customer initiates each minute with probability ½.

Suppose that the cost of origination as well as the cost of termination equals 1, and that carriers set usage rates equal to this cost plus access. (When $a = 0$ all usage rates equal 1. When $a = 1$, on-net usage rates equal 1, off-net origination rates equal 2, and off-net termination rates $= 0$.)

Proposition 6. If for every $v' \in [0, v]$ the distribution of the allocation of the value of a minute between the parties is symmetric and single peaked,[38] then $a = 0$ leads to a more efficient utilization of the network than does $a = 1$. Further if for every v' the distribution is symmetric and has greater weight in the tails,[39] then $a = 1$ is more efficient than $a = 0$.[40]

Proof: The formal proof is provided in Appendix A.

This proposition is the natural extension of Proposition 3. It says essentially that, if the value of most of the minutes is shared roughly evenly between the two parties, then allocating the cost evenly between the parties will be more efficient than assigning all of the costs to the caller. This is because if the value of most minutes is divided roughly evenly between the two parties,

---

[37] Some may argue that no one would ever initiate a call for which he received no benefit and that therefore 0 and small values around 0 should be excluded. However, this same argument implies that a called party who received no benefit would never engage in a call, so small values around 1 should also be eliminated.

[38] A distribution is single peaked if it is increasing for values less than the mean and decreasing for all values greater than the mean.

[39] A distribution has more weight in the tails if is decreasing for values less than the mean and increasing for all values greater than the mean.

then bill and keep causes only the small fraction of minutes, ones for which one party receives most of the benefit, (and for which total benefit is slightly larger than total incremental cost) to not be consumed. Imposing all of the cost on the calling party however, cause a larger fraction of minutes, ones for which the benefit is relatively evenly divided between the parties (and for which total benefit is slightly larger than total incremental cost) not to be consumed. Conversely, if primarily one party or the other enjoys most of the value of each minute, imposing all of the cost on the calling party will be relatively more efficient.

This intuition can be extended to compare the surplus from $a = 0$ to the surplus when a is any positive number, and show that $a = 0$ always yields greater surplus. Thus we have the following:

Corollary 1. If for every v' the distribution of the allocation of the value is symmetric and single peaked, then $a = 0$ is second best optimal among linear termination rates.

4.3. Inter-carrier compensation and regulated retail rates

U.S. regulators typically require ILECs to offer residential service on a flat-rated basis.[41] When carriers use only flat-rated charges, per minute access costs are not passed on as per minute retail rates and, thus, do not affect short run usage decisions. Rather, they simply transfer wealth between carriers.

Suppose carriers cannot distinguish A from B and so must set the same flat-rated charge to each customer.[42] Suppose that $c_1 = c_2 = c/2$, and that each customer engages in m_0 minutes of conversation when facing a zero usage rate. Competition drives the flat rate down to $m_0c/2$, the

---

[40] See Figure 2 for a graph of each distribution.
[41] Exceptions include Chicago and parts of New York City, which have metered residential service.
[42] Restricting one carrier to set flat-rated rates while the other to sets usage rates induces an equilibrium in which the carrier that sets usage rates serves all of the customers, because he can set rates efficiently.

expected average total cost generated by a customer. In this case $a = 0$ ensures that every carrier earns a zero profit, regardless of the balance of traffic between networks.

If $a = c/2$, then although ex-ante both carriers earn a zero profit, because customers are chosen randomly to originate calls, ex-post there is a positive probability that traffic will be unbalanced. The network that originates more off-net traffic than it terminates will earn a loss, and the network that terminates more off-net traffic than it originates will earn a profit. Thus, termination charges add variance to carriers' profit without affecting the expected value. Assuming variance in income is to be avoided, bill and keep is desirable regardless of the balance of traffic, and cost-based termination is less desirable if traffic is unbalanced.

Now assume both carriers could price discriminate between customers based on the share of minutes they originate. Equilibrium prices ensure that each customer generates a zero expected profit. With $a = 0$, in equilibrium each customer would face a flat rate of $m_0c/2$. When $a = c/2$, the flat-rated charge for A would be $(7/12)m_0c$,[43] and the flat-rated charge for B would be $(5/12)m_0c$. Each customer would cover the full marginal cost of the expected proportion of calls he initiated. However, even with price discrimination, $a = c/2$ still generates variance in carriers' income.

A second problem with $a = c/2$ is that it could lead to cross-subsidization. Suppose ISPs only receive calls, because they only provide dial-up service. Suppose all residential customers subscriber to the ILEC.[44] All residential customers consume the same number of minutes, but some use dial-up Internet service and others only speak with other customers on the ILEC network. A single residential subscription rate applies to all residential customers, and for simplicity there are only marginal costs of serving customers and no fixed costs.

---

[43] Assuming customers choose each carrier with probability ½, when A subscribes to Carrier 1 there is a ½ probability that B will be on network 2. So A originates an off-net call with probability ½ x ⅔ and when he does so, he imposes a cost of m_0c on Carrier 1. When he receives a call, the cost he imposes on Carrier 1 is just offset by the termination charge Carrier 1 receives. There is also a ½ probability that B also subscribes to network 1, in which case each customer imposes a cost of $m_0c/2$ on the carrier. Thus A imposes an expected cost of $(7/12)m_0c$ on Carrier 1.
[44] As of this writing, ILECs provided over 98% of residential wireline service in the United States.

Under $a = c/2$, competition would drive the retail price paid by ISPs to 0, since a carrier that serves an ISP receives access revenue that covers the full cost of serving the ISP. The ILEC, who serves all of the residential customers, pays for all these access revenues if the ISP is served by the CLEC. Because there is a single residential rate, these costs are averaged across all residential customers, whether or not they use the Internet. Thus non-Internet users subsidize those customers who use the Internet.

This problem is mitigated under $a = 0$. In this case, the cost of switching and half of the transport is imposed directly on the ISP, which would then be recovered in the ISP's subscription rates. Thus, only customers who use the ISP would pay for these costs. Here, only the other half of the transport costs would be averaged into the residential rates.

5. Conclusion

In this paper I have examined the effect of an inter-carrier compensation regime on market performance. I have shown that the compensation rate should be viewed as a way of dividing the incremental cost of the facilities needed to complete an off-net call between the parties. This is different from the current practice and literature, in which the inter-carrier compensation rate is viewed as the price of inputs the originating network purchases from the terminating network when it "sells completed calls" to the calling party.

The main result is that it is efficient for each customer to bear the proportion of the incremental cost of a call equal to the proportion of the value of the call he receives. MBAK results in retail rates that divide the cost of the call evenly when carriers employ the same technology and competition drives retail rates to cost. This is efficient when customers shared equally in the value of a call. Additionally, CPNP results in a socially inefficient pricing structure that cause underutilization and underdeployment of facilities relative to the social optimum unless the calling party receives all of the benefit of a call.

Second, CPNP can create a tipping effect. That is, because it overallocates the cost of off-net calls to the calling party, all customers have an incentive to cluster on the same network. While such a result may be efficient in a static sense, it would seem counterproductive in a market like telecommunications in which viable competitors are being introduced as a way to eliminate the need for regulation.

Appendix A

Proof of Proposition 3.

Under the proposed equilibrium customers subscribe randomly to each network. The customers engage in 3 minutes of conversation, because for each party the benefit of the 3rd minute is $(1/2)(5-3) = 1$. Each party receives a surplus of 2.25 (calculated as a total benefit of 5.25 less total usage payments of 3).

Define the surplus earned by customer j as S_{jii}, $j \in \{A, B\}$ where the first i subscript indicates A subscribes to network i and the second i subscript indicates B's subscription choice. The following rules are subgame perfect responses for customers.

If for only one carrier, Carrier i, prices are such that, $S_{Aii} > S_{A-ii}$ and $S_{Bii} > S_{Bi-i}$, then both customers subscribe to network i.

If for both carriers, prices are such that $S_{Aii} > S_{A-ii}$ and $S_{Bii} > S_{Bi-i}$ then if $\Sigma_j S_{jii} > \Sigma_j S_{j-i-i}$ each customer subscribes to network i, and if $\Sigma_j S_{jii} < \Sigma_j S_{j-i-i}$ then each customer subscribes to network $-i$.

If for both carriers, prices are such that $S_{Aii} > S_{A-ii}$ and $S_{Bii} > S_{Bi-i}$ and $\Sigma_j S_{jii} = \Sigma_j S_{j-i-i}$ but $\Sigma_j S_{jii}$ is greater than the sum of customers' surplus if one customer subscribes to each network, then subscribe to network 1.

Lemmas 1 and 2 now rule out all possible deviations by a carrier.

Lemma 1. Assume WOLG that Carrier 2 deviates from the proposed equilibrium. No deviation in which Carrier 2 sets either $p_{2of} \leq 1$ or $p_{2tf} \leq 1$ can be a profitable deviation.

Proof. Suppose that there is a deviation in which $p_{2tf} \leq 1$. If A subscribes to network 1, he earns an expected surplus of 2.25 regardless of the network to which B subscribes. This is because if $p_{2tf} \leq 1$, and B subscribes to network 2, B is willing to terminate (at least) 3 minutes worth of calls. Therefore if A subscribes to network 1, he can engage in 3 minutes of conversation with B regardless of the network to which B subscribes, and pay 1 cent per minute for each minute.[45] That is, if B is chosen as the initiator of the call and $p_{2of} > 1$, B will originate the call, but not consume 3 minutes of conversation (because the origination rate exceeds 1). However, A will then originate a call (since his origination rate equals 1), and B will terminate the call (since his termination rate is less than or equal to 1) and the parties will consume minutes to the point where the minutes from the initial call and the second call equal 3. Similarly, if Carrier 2 sets $p_{2of} \leq 1$, B is willing to originate (at least) 3 minutes. Thus, if A is chosen as the initiator of the first call and B faces a termination rate greater than 1, the initial call will not last 3 minutes but B will then initiate a call that covers the balance of the time.

Therefore, in any subgame perfect continuation in which Carrier 2 sets either her off-net origination rates or her off-net termination rate less than 1, any customer that subscribes to network 2 must earn a payoff at least as great as 2.25. Suppose such a customer subscribes to network 2 and engages in 3 minutes of conversation. Then to earn a surplus of at least 2.25, he must pay total usage fees that total no more than 3. Since he generates a cost of 3, Carrier 2 could never earn a positive profit from such a customer.

I know show that no customer can subscribe to network 2 and consume a quantity of minutes other than 3 and earn a surplus greater than 2.25 while Carrier 2 earns a 0 payoff. A customer that consumes m minutes receives a benefit of $[2.5 - m/4]m$. Letting U be total usage payments, the customer's surplus would be $[2.5 - m/4]m - U$. If Carrier 2 earned a zero payoff, then she would have to receive usage payments equal to m. Thus, the customer's surplus would equal $[2.5 - m/4]m - m$. The m that maximizes this expression is $m = 3$. Thus, a customer cannot earn a surplus higher than 2.25 while the carrier earns a zero payoff.

---

[45] Thus, if the customer on network 2 is chosen to originate a call to the customer on network 1, but faces an off-net origination rate greater than the private benefit for some minutes less than 3, then the customer on

Lemma 2. No deviation in which Carrier 2 sets $p_{2of} > 1$ and $p_{2tf} > 1$ can be a subgame perfect profitable deviation.

Proof. Because $p_{2of} > 1$ and $p_{2tf} > 1$, if both customers were to subscribe to network 1, no customer could subscribe to network 2 by himself and earn a surplus in excess of 2.25. All minutes for such a customer would be off-net so they would all be priced above 1, and because of this the customer would consume fewer than 3 minutes. Thus we need only consider continuations in which all customers subscribe to network 2 in response to a deviation by carrier 2.

Both customers will subscribe to network 2 only if the sum of their surpluses is at least 4.5 = (2x2.25). Then it must be the case that any customer earning a surplus of 2.25 pays no more than the cost he imposes on Carrier 2, and any customer that earns a surplus greater than 2.25 must pay less than the cost he imposes on Carrier 2. Thus, such a deviation cannot result in a positive profit for Carrier 2.

Lemmas 1 and 2 rule out all possible deviations. Thus, the proposed equilibrium is an equilibrium. In this equilibrium customers consume minutes up to the point where the marginal benefit to society equals the marginal cost to society, thus maximizing social surplus. Thus, this equilibrium is efficient. *QED.*

Proof of Proposition 5

Suppose each carrier sets the prices proposed in the proposition.

Lemma 3. The customers' strategies described in Proposition 4 are also subgame perfect in this game.

Proof. Because these strategies are subgame perfect and independent of prices set by the carriers, they constitute subgame perfect behavior when $a = 1$.

---

network 1 will originate any minutes up to 3 that were not consumed in the original call.

Lemma 4. The only subgame perfect response to the prices proposed in the proposition is for both customers to subscribe to the same network.

Proof. If both customers subscribe to network 1, each earns a surplus of 2.25, consuming 3 minutes of calling for a benefit of 5.25, and paying 3 in switching costs. Suppose *B* subscribed network 2. With probability 1/3 he will originate the call, and with probability 2/3 he will terminate the call. In either case he will consume only 1 minute of calling (which results in a benefit of 2.25). His expected surplus from subscribing to network 2 is only 1.583 = (1/3)(2.25 - 2) + (2/3)(2.25-0).

A similar calculation shows that at these prices, *A* cannot earn a higher surplus by subscribing to network 2 while *B* subscribes to network 1.

Lemmas 3 and 4 show that in response to the prices proposed in the proposition, the only subgame perfect response is for both customers to subscribe to the same network. I now show there is no deviation by a carrier that allows her to earn a strictly positive profit.

Suppose WLOG both customers subscribe to network 1. In this equilibrium both carriers earn 0.

Lemma 5. If Carrier 2 were to deviate so that there were a subgame perfect continuation in which one or both of the customers subscribed to her network, she could not earn a positive profit.

Proof. Suppose Carrier 2 deviates by setting on-net rates low enough so that $\Sigma_j S_{j22} > \Sigma_j S_{j11}$ $j \in \{A, B\}$ Then the customers must jointly receive a surplus of 4.5. But since the maximum joint customer surplus is 4.5 when a carrier earns a profit of 0 (Lemma 1), there can be no continuation in which both customers subscribe to network 2 and earn a joint surplus in excess of 4.5, that allows Carrier 2 to earn a strictly positive profit.

Now, let Carrier 2 sets off-net prices so that just one customer subscribes to network 2.

The most surplus one customer could earn by subscribing to network 2 subject to Carrier 2 earning a non-negative profit would occur if $p_{2of} > 2.5$ and $p_{2tf} = 0$. In this case the customer on network 2 would never originate a call and would receive 1 minute of calling, earning a surplus of 2.25. At these prices Carrier 2 would earn a zero profit. Thus there is no deviation in which one customer would choose to subscribe to Carrier 2 that allows Carrier 2 to earn a positive profit.

QED

Proof of Proposition 6

For any valuation, v', define the statistic $D_{v'}$ which is the difference between the calling party's individual valuation and the called party's individual valuation. $D_{v'}$ is distributed on the interval $[-v', v']$, where $D_{v'} = -v'$ means the called party receives all of the value and $D_{v'} = v'$ means the calling party receives all the value. The conditions of the proposition imply that for each v' the distribution of $D_{v'}$ is symmetric about zero.

I now show graphically in Figure 1. that for each v' $a = 0$ results in more minutes being consumed than $a = 1$ when the distribution of $D_{v'}$ is single peaked. The graph measures the calling party's value of a minute on the horizontal axis and the called party's valuation of a minute on the vertical axis. Let v_o represent the calling party's valuation and v_t represent the called party's valuation. The locus $v_o + v_t = v'$ for $0 < v_o < v'$ and $0 < v_t < v'$ and $0 < v' < v$ represents all of the possible divisions of the value of a minute that the parties value jointly at v'. This locus is a line with slope -1 and an intercept of v'.

When $a = 0$, and all originating and terminating minutes are priced at 1 (the cost of switching), all minutes are consumed for which $v_o \geq 1$ and $v_t \geq 1$, which is given by the locus of points "north east" of (1, 1) (Point T in Figure 1). When $a = 1$ and prices are symmetric in equilibrium, the usage rate for originated off-net minutes is 2, the usage rate for terminating off-net minutes is 0 and the usage rate for all on-net minutes is 1. All of the minutes northeast of (2, 1), (Point W in Figure 1) are consumed. In addition ½ of the minutes in trapezoid $TUVW$ are consumed and ½ of the minutes in trapezoid $WXYZ$ are consumed. (This is because ½ of the minutes in trapezoid $TUVW$ are on-net minutes and ½ are off-net. In the $a=1$ equilibrium, only the on-net minutes in $TUVW$ are consumed. Similarly, ½ the minutes in $WXYZ$ are off-net minutes and ½ are on-net minutes, and in the $a=0$ equilibrium only the off-net minutes are consumed.) Therefore, switching from $a=0$ to $a=1$ means eliminating half of the minutes in trapezoid $TUVW$ and adding half the minutes in trapezoid $WXYZ$.

I must show that the value of the minutes represented by trapezoid $TUVW$ is greater than the value of the minutes represented by trapezoid $WXYZ$ to show that $a=0$ results in an equilibrium with greater surplus than from $a=1$. First, every line of the form $v_o + v_t = v'$ that passes through trapezoid $TUVW$ also passes through $WXYZ$ and vice versa. Second, these two trapezoids have the same dimensions. Third, the length of the segment of any line that passes through $TUVW$ is the same length as the segment of that line that passes through $WXYZ$. Thus, to compare the number of minutes represented by two such line segments, I need only compare the density of minutes associated with each of the line segments. Because the distribution is symmetric, increasing for $v_o > v_t$ and decreasing for $v_o < v_t$, and because $TUVW$ is closer to the center of any line of the form $v_o + v_t = v'$ than is $WXYZ$, the density along any line segment that passes through $TUVW$ must be greater than its counterpart that passes through $WXYZ$. Thus, the density in $TUVW$ must be greater than the density in $WXYZ$, so $a=0$ is more efficient than $a=1$.

Similarly, if for every v' the distribution is symmetric, but has greater weight in the tails, then the density in $WXYZ$ is greater than the density in $TUVW$, so $a=1$ is more efficient than $a=0$.

QED

References

Atkinson, Jay, and Christopher Barnekov, 2000, "A Competitively Neutral Approach to Network Interconnection," Federal Communications Commission, OPP Working Paper # 34, Released December.

Besen, Stanley, Willard Maning, and Bridger Mitchell, 1978, "Copyright Liability for Cable Television: Compulsory Licensing and the Coase Theorem," *Journal of Law and Economics*, vol. XXI, April, pp. 67-95.

Brennan, Timothy, 1997, "Industry Parallel Interconnection Agreements," *Information Economics and Policy*, pp 133-149.

DeGraba, Patrick, 2000, "Efficient Interconnection for Competing Networks," Mimeo.

DeGraba, Patrick, 2002, "Central Office Bill and Keep as a Unified Inter-Carrier Compensation Regime," *Yale Journal on Regulation*, 19 (1) pp. 39-84.

Doyle, Chris, and Jennifer Smith, 1998, "Market Structure in Mobile Telecoms: Qualified Indirect Access and the Receiver Pays Principle," *Information Economics and Policy*, 10, pp. 471-88.

Economides, Nicholas, Giuseppe Lopomo, and Glenn Woroch, 1996, "Strategic Commitments and the Principle of Reciprocity in Interconnection Pricing," Discussion Paper EC-96-13, Stern School of Business, N.Y.U.

Federal Communications Commission, 1996, *Local Competition Order*, First Report and Order, 11 FCC Rcd. 15499.

Gans, Joshua, and Stephen King, 2001, "The Neutrality of Interchange Fees in Payment Systems," University of Melbourne Working Paper.

Hermalin, B. and M. Katz , "Network Interconnection with Two-Sided User Benefits," July 2001 mimeo.

Katz, M., G. Rosston, and J. Anspacher, 1995, "Interconnecting Interoperable Systems: The Regulators' Perspective," *Information, Infrastructure and Policy*, 4 , pp. 327-342.

Kim, Jeong Yoo and Yoonsung Lim, 2001, "An Economic Analysis of the Receiver Pays Principle," *Information Economics and Policy* 12, pp. 231-260.

Laffont, Jean-Jacques and Jean Tirole, 2000, *Competition in Telecommunications*, Cambridge MA, MIT Press Cambridge, MA.

Laffont, Jean-Jacques, Patrick Rey and Jean Tirole, 1998, "Network Competition: II. Price Discrimination, " *RAND Journal of Economics*, 29, (1) pp. 38-56.

Salop, Steven, 1990, "Deregulating Self Regulated Shared ATM Networks," *Econ. Innov. New Techn.*, 1, pp. 85-96.

Sidak, Gregory, and Daniel Spulber, 1996, "Deregulatory Takings and Breach of the Regulatory Contract," *New York University Law Review*, 40, pp. 61-90.

Squire, Lyn, 1973, "Some Aspects of Optimal Pricing for Telecommunications," *Bell Journal of Economics*, 4, 2, pp. 515-525.

Willig, Robert, 1979, "The Theory of Network Access Pricing," in *Issues in Public Utility Regulation,* ed. by H. Tribing, East Lansing, Mich. St. Univ.

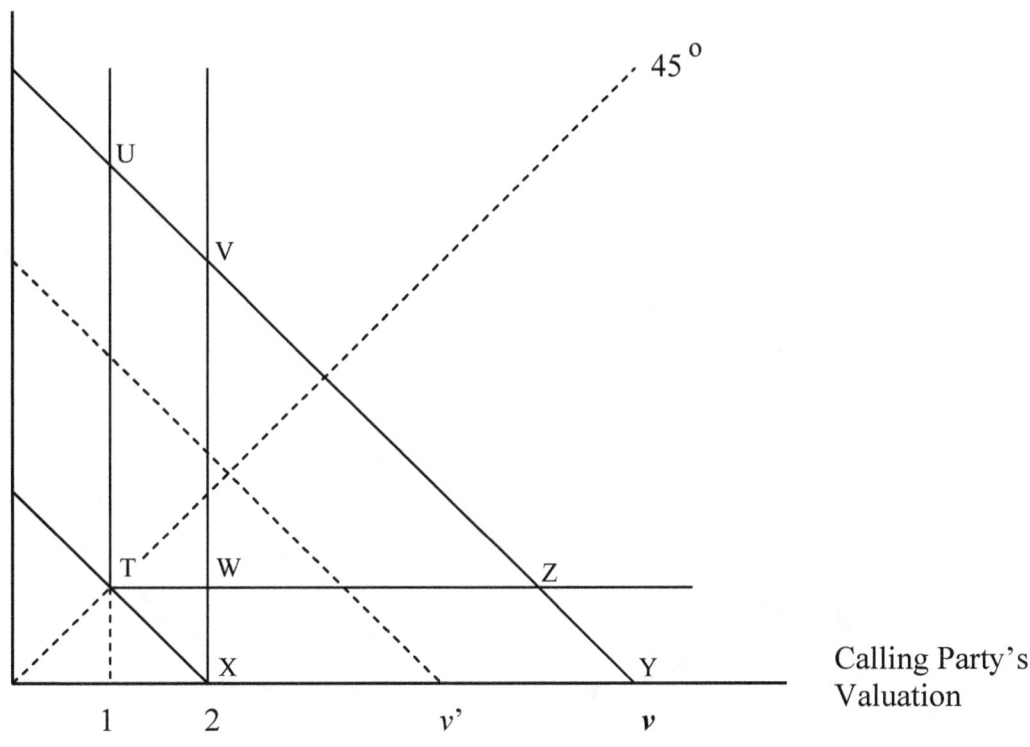

Figure 1.

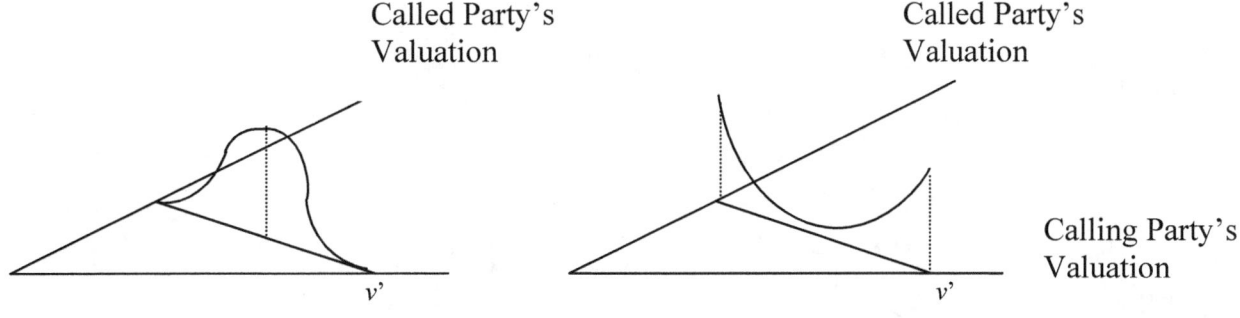

Figure 2
A single peaked distribution of the allocation of all minutes with value v', and a distribution of the allocation of all minutes with value v' with more weight in the tails.